How Do I Pay All My Bills?

Mastering Velocity

Banking and Financial

Management

H.N. Williams

Chapter One: Introduction to Velocity Banking

Velocity Banking and Basic Principles

Velocity banking is a financial strategy that uses various lines of credit, such as a Home Equity Line of Credit (HELOC), a Personal Line of Credit (PLOC), or a zero-interest credit card, to pay off high-interest debt quickly and efficiently. The core idea is to optimize cash flow by strategically using borrowed funds, reducing overall interest payments, and accelerating debt repayment. This approach allows individuals to leverage their income more effectively and achieve financial freedom faster.

How Velocity Banking Differs from Traditional Banking

Traditional banking methods involve paying off debts slowly over time, often resulting in high interest costs. In contrast, velocity banking emphasizes rapid debt reduction by using a revolving line of credit. This difference is akin to taking the scenic route versus the fast lane. Velocity banking focuses on maintaining positive cash flow, whereas traditional banking may not prioritize this aspect, leading to more efficient debt management and faster financial progress.

Benefits of Velocity Banking

Velocity banking offers several benefits, including reduced interest payments, quicker debt payoff, and improved cash flow management. By reducing the principal balance faster, individuals can save significant amounts on interest, freeing up money for other financial goals. This method also provides greater flexibility in managing finances, allowing for faster wealth accumulation and financial stability.

Real-World Applications

Many individuals and families have successfully implemented velocity banking to improve their financial health. For example, my family used a HELOC to pay off our credit card debts, resulting in substantial interest savings and quicker debt elimination. By following a structured approach, I was able to redirect our income towards debt repayment, achieving financial freedom much faster!

Common Misconceptions

There are several misconceptions about velocity banking, such as it being too complicated or risky. With proper understanding and disciplined management, velocity banking can be a highly effective strategy. It's essential to debunk myths and educate individuals on the practical steps and benefits of this approach, ensuring they make informed financial decisions.

Chapter 2: The Basics of Financial Management

Importance of Financial Management

Financial management is crucial for achieving stability and security. It involves planning, organizing, and controlling financial activities to ensure efficient use of resources. Effective financial management helps individuals make informed decisions, avoid debt, and save for future needs. It is the foundation for building a secure financial future and achieving long-term goals.

Key Financial Principles: Budgeting, Saving and Investing

Budgeting is the process of creating a plan for how to spend and save money. It involves tracking income, expenses, and setting limits to avoid overspending. A well-structured budget helps manage finances effectively, ensuring that all essential expenses are covered while allowing for savings and investments.

Saving is essential for financial security and future needs. Setting aside a portion of income regularly helps build an emergency fund and prepare for unexpected expenses. Savings can also be used for larger financial goals, such as buying a home, education, or retirement.

Investing involves putting money into assets with the potential to grow in value over time. It includes stocks, bonds, real estate, and other investment vehicles. Investing helps build wealth and provides financial growth opportunities beyond regular savings.

Setting Financial Goals

Setting financial goals is like creating a roadmap for your financial journey. Goals can be short-term, like saving for a vacation, or long-term, like buying a home. Effective goal setting involves making them Specific, Measurable, Achievable, Relevant, and Time-bound (SMART). This approach ensures clarity and motivation to achieve financial objectives.

Chapter 3: Setting Up Your Financial Foundation

Creating a Budget

Creating a budget involves listing all sources of income and detailing all expenses, from essentials like rent and groceries to discretionary spending like entertainment. Start by tracking your spending for a month to get a clear picture of where your money goes. Then, categorize your expenses and set limits for each category. This helps ensure that you live within your means and prioritize savings.

Building an Emergency Fund

An emergency fund is a savings account set aside for unexpected expenses, like medical bills or car repairs. Aim to save enough to cover three to six months of living expenses. Start small by saving a portion of your income each month until you reach your goal. Having an emergency fund provides a financial safety net, reducing stress and financial strain during emergencies.

Managing Expenses

Managing expenses involves tracking spending habits and adjusting to avoid overspending. Use tools like expense tracking apps to monitor your spending in real-time. Identify areas where you can cut back, such as dining out or subscription services, and redirect those funds towards savings and debt repayment. Effective expense management helps maintain financial stability and supports long-term financial goals.

Chapter 4: Understanding Debt

Types of Debt

   Good Debt: Good debt is borrowed money used for investments that increase in value or generate long-term income, such as student loans or mortgages. These types of debt are considered beneficial as they contribute to personal and financial growth.

Bad Debt: Bad debt is borrowed money used for items that do not increase in value or generate income, such as credit card debt for non-essential purchases. This type of debt can be detrimental to financial health due to high-interest rates and minimal return on investment.

How Debt Affects Your Financial Health

Debt can impact your financial health in various ways. High-interest debt can lead to increased financial stress and limit your ability to save and invest. It can also affect your credit score, which influences your ability to borrow money on favorable terms. Managing debt effectively is crucial for maintaining financial stability and achieving long-term goals.

Strategies for Managing and Reducing Debt

Debt Repayment Methods: There are various methods to pay off debt, such as the snowball method (paying off smaller debts first) and the avalanche method (paying off debts with the highest interest rates first). Choose a method that suits your financial situation and stick to it consistently.

Consolidation and Refinancing: Consolidating multiple debts into a single loan with a lower interest rate can simplify repayment and reduce overall interest costs. Refinancing high-interest debt, like credit cards, into lower-interest loans can also help save money and accelerate debt repayment.

Chapter 5: The Concept of Cash Flow

Importance of Positive Cash Flow

Positive cash flow means you have more money coming in than going out. It is crucial for financial health, as it allows you to cover expenses, save for future needs, and invest in opportunities. Positive cash flow provides financial flexibility and reduces the risk of falling into debt.

Analyzing Your Cash Flow

To analyze your cash flow, track all sources of income and expenses over a period, typically a month. Create a cash flow statement that lists all income and expenses and calculate the net cash flow (income minus expenses). Identify trends and areas where you can improve, such as reducing unnecessary expenses or increasing income sources

Improving Cash Flow with Velocity Banking

Velocity banking helps improve cash flow by using a line of credit to pay off high-interest debts quickly. This reduces monthly interest payments and frees up more money for other expenses. By maintaining positive cash flow, you can manage your finances more effectively and achieve financial goals faster.

Chapter 6: Leveraging Credit Cards and Lines of Credit

Using Credit Cards Effectively

Credit cards can be a useful financial tool if used wisely. Pay off the balance in full each month to avoid interest charges and build a positive credit history. Take advantage of rewards programs and cashback offers to maximize benefits. Avoid using credit cards for non-essential purchases that you cannot pay off immediately.

Understanding Lines of Credit

A line of credit is a flexible loan that allows you to borrow up to a certain limit. It differs from a traditional loan because you only pay interest on the amount you borrow. Lines of credit can be used for various purposes, such as consolidating debt, covering emergencies, or making large purchases. Managing a line of credit responsibly can help improve cash flow and financial stability.

How to Use Them in Velocity Banking

In velocity banking, lines of credit are used to pay off high-interest debts quickly. By borrowing from a line of credit with a lower interest rate, you can reduce overall interest costs and accelerate debt repayment. Use extra income to pay down the line of credit balance, maintaining positive cash flow and financial flexibility.

Chapter 7: Implementing the Velocity Banking Strategy

Steps to Implement Velocity Banking

Implementing velocity banking involves several key steps:

- ★ *Assess Your Finances*: Start by evaluating your income, expenses, and debts. Create a detailed list of all your financial obligations and categorize them by interest rates and amounts.

- *Set Up Necessary Accounts*: Open a HELOC or line of credit if you don't already have one. This will be your primary tool for managing and paying off debts.
- *Develop a Debt Repayment Plan*: Prioritize high-interest debts for immediate repayment using the funds from your line of credit. Make a list of which debts to tackle first and how much to pay towards each.
- *Maintain Positive Cash Flow*: Ensure your monthly income exceeds your expenses. Use

any surplus income to pay down the line of credit as quickly as possible.

★ *Monitor and Adjust*: Regularly review your financial progress and adjust your strategy as needed. Keep track of your debt reduction and make necessary changes to stay on track.

Using HELOC (Home Equity Line of Credit)

A Home Equity Line of Credit (HELOC) is a loan that uses the equity in your home as collateral. It offers a flexible borrowing option that you can use as needed, similar to a credit card but with typically lower interest rates. Here's how to use a HELOC in velocity banking:

- *Apply for a HELOC*: Contact your bank or lender to apply for a HELOC. Ensure you understand the terms and conditions, including the interest rate and repayment schedule.
- *Pay Off High-Interest Debt*: Use the HELOC funds to pay off high-interest debts like credit cards. This reduces the overall interest you pay.
- *Focus on Repayment*: Each month, allocate as much of your income as possible to repay the

HELOC balance. This will free up the credit line for future use and reduce your debt more quickly.

Practical Examples and Case Studies

Example 1: The Johnson Family: The Johnson family had $15,000 in credit card debt with an interest rate of 20%. By using their HELOC, which had a 5% interest rate, they paid off the credit card balance and redirected their income to repay the HELOC. Within two years, they cleared the debt and saved thousands in interest.

Example 2: The Lee Household: The Lee household used velocity banking to pay off their car loan and personal loans. They consistently monitored their cash flow and adjusted their repayment plan as needed. By prioritizing debt repayment with their HELOC, they achieved financial stability much faster than using traditional methods.

Chapter 8: How to Pay All My Bills with Velocity Banking

In this chapter, we'll dive into a powerful strategy for paying all your bills and managing debt more effectively. The method revolves around using a chosen line of credit to manage your income and expenses, reducing your debt faster and optimizing cash flow. Let's break it down step-by-step.

Step 1: Setting Up Your Accounts

To begin, you'll need the following accounts:

1. <u>Primary Checking Account</u>: For direct payments such as mortgage, HOA, and insurance.
2. <u>Line of Credit</u> (HELOC, PLOC, or zero interest credit card): This will be used to pay down debt and manage other monthly expenses.

Step 2: Deposit Your Income

Deposit *all your income* into your chosen line of credit, *except* for the amount needed to cover direct payments from your checking account. For example, if your monthly income is $5,000 and your mortgage, HOA, and insurance total $2,000, deposit the remaining $3,000 into the line of credit.

Step 3: Pay Down the Line of Credit

By depositing the majority of your income into the line of credit, you immediately reduce the outstanding balance. This decreases the interest accruing on the line of credit, saving you money over time.

Step 4: Cover Monthly Expenses

Use the line of credit to pay for all your monthly expenses, such as groceries, utilities, and other bills. This way, you're essentially recycling the same funds while keeping your cash flow optimized.

Step 5: Direct Payments from Checking Account

Ensure that you have enough funds in your primary checking account to cover direct payments like mortgage, HOA, and insurance. Transfer the necessary amount from your income before depositing the rest into the line of credit.

Step 6: Rinse and Repeat

Continue this cycle each month:

1. Deposit your income (minus direct payment amounts) into the line of credit.
2. Use the line of credit to cover monthly expenses. (Set up auto-pay, so you're never late on a payment.)
3. Direct payments are made from your checking account.

Over time, this method allows you to:

- ✓ <u>Reduce Debt Faster</u>: By constantly lowering the balance on your line of credit, you reduce the interest paid and accelerate debt repayment.

- ✓ <u>Optimize Cash Flow</u>: Keeping your money actively working for you means you have more flexibility and control over your finances.

- ✓ <u>Achieve Financial Freedom</u>: As your debt decreases, you move closer to financial independence.

Practical Example

Let's consider an example to illustrate this method:

Scenario:

- Monthly Income: $5,000
- Direct Payments (Mortgage, HOA, Insurance): $2,000
- Line of Credit Balance: $10,000
- Monthly Expenses: $3,000

Steps:

1. Deposit $3,000 into the line of credit, reducing the balance to $7,000.
2. Use the line of credit to pay for $3,000 worth of monthly expenses, bringing the balance back to $10,000.
3. Ensure $2,000 remains in the checking account to cover direct payments.

Each month, repeat this process. Over time, as the principal on the line of credit reduces, you save on interest payments and free up more of your income.

Key Points to Remember

- ☺ <u>Consistency is Key</u>: Stick to the plan and repeat the cycle each month to see the best results.
- ☺ <u>Monitor Your Accounts</u>: Regularly review your line of credit and checking account balances to ensure you're on track.
- ☺ <u>Adjust as Needed</u>: If your income or expenses change, adjust the amounts deposited and used from the line of credit accordingly.

By following these steps, you can effectively manage your bills, reduce debt, and move towards financial freedom with confidence.

Chapter 9: Advanced Financial Strategies

Investing Basics

Investing is the process of putting money into assets that have the potential to grow in value over time. Common investment options include stocks, bonds, real estate, and mutual funds. Here are some key points to understand:

Risk and Return: Investments come with varying levels of risk and potential return. Higher-risk investments often offer higher returns, while lower-risk investments provide more stability.

Diversification: Spread your investments across different asset classes to reduce risk. This means not putting all your eggs in one basket.

Some Types of Investments:

- ★ *Stocks*: Shares of ownership in a company.

- *Bonds*: Loans you give to companies or governments that pay you interest over time.
- *Real Estate*: Property ownership that can generate rental income or appreciate in value.
- *Mutual Funds*: Pools of money from many investors used to buy a diversified portfolio of stocks, bonds, or other assets.

Tax Planning and Strategies

Tax planning involves organizing your finances in a way that minimizes your tax liability.

Effective tax planning can save you money and maximize your income. Here are some strategies:

- *Understand Tax Deductions and Credits*: Familiarize yourself with tax deductions and credits available to you. These can reduce the amount of tax you owe.

- *Retirement Accounts*: Contribute to retirement accounts like IRAs or 401(k)s, which offer tax advantages. These accounts can reduce your taxable income and grow tax-deferred until retirement.

- *Tax-Efficient Investments*: Choose investments that provide tax benefits, such as municipal bonds that are often tax-exempt at the federal level.

Building Wealth Over Time

Building wealth is a long-term process that involves consistent saving, investing, and smart financial planning. Here are key steps to build wealth:

- *Start Early*: The earlier you start saving and investing, the more time your money has to grow. Compound interest can significantly increase your wealth over time.

- *Set Clear Goals*: Define your financial goals, such as buying a home, funding education, or retiring comfortably. Create a plan to achieve these goals.
- *Stay Disciplined*: Regularly contribute to your savings and investment accounts. Avoid unnecessary expenses and stick to your financial plan.

How Do I Pay All My Bills? Mastering Velocity Banking and Financial Management

Chapter 10: Monitoring and Adjusting Your Plan

Tracking Your Financial Progress

Regularly monitoring your financial progress is essential for staying on track and achieving your goals. Here's how to do it:

- ★ *Review Financial Statements*: Periodically review your bank statements, credit card statements, and investment account statements. Look for patterns and areas where you can improve.

- *Use Financial Tracking Tools*: Utilize apps and software designed to track your spending, saving, and investing. These tools can provide valuable insights and help you stay organized.
- *Set Milestones*: Establish financial milestones to measure your progress. For example, aim to save a certain amount each quarter or reduce your debt by a specific percentage.

Adjusting Your Strategy as Needed

Life circumstances and financial markets can change, requiring adjustments to your financial strategy. Here are some tips:

- *Reevaluate Goals*: Periodically reassess your financial goals to ensure they are still relevant and achievable. Adjust them based on changes in your life or financial situation.
- *Adapt to Market Changes*: Stay informed about economic and market trends. Be prepared to

adjust your investment strategy if necessary to protect your assets or take advantage of new opportunities.

- ★ *Seek Professional Advice*: Consider consulting with a financial advisor to review your plan and provide guidance. Professional advice can help you make informed decisions and stay on track.

Tools and Resources for Financial Management

Several tools and resources can assist with effective financial management:

- ★ *Budgeting Apps*: Apps like Mint, YNAB (You Need a Budget), and Pocket Guard help you track expenses, create budgets, and manage money more efficiently.
- ★ *Investment Platforms*: Platforms like Robinhood, E*TRADE, and Vanguard

allow you to invest in stocks, bonds, and other assets with ease.

- ★ *Educational Resources*: Books, online courses, and financial blogs offer valuable information and tips on managing finances. Websites like Investopedia and NerdWallet provide comprehensive financial education.

Chapter 11: Building a Financially Secure Future

Long-term Financial Planning

Long-term financial planning is essential for achieving your future financial goals and ensuring stability. It involves creating a strategy that spans many years, allowing you to save, invest, and grow your wealth over time.

Assess Your Current Situation Start by taking a comprehensive look at your current financial situation. This includes understanding your income, expenses, debts, and assets. Create a detailed financial statement to get a clear picture of where you stand.

Define Long-term Goals Set specific long-term goals, such as buying a home, funding education, or retiring comfortably. Make these goals SMART: Specific, Measurable, Achievable, Relevant, and Time-bound. For example, instead of saying "I want to save for retirement," specify "I want to save $1 million by the age of 65."

Develop a Plan Once you have your goals, create a detailed plan outlining the steps to achieve them. This includes budgeting, saving, investing, and debt management strategies. Your plan should be realistic and flexible to adapt to changes in your financial situation or goals.

Review and Adjust Regularly review your financial plan to ensure you are on track to achieve your goals. Adjust your plan as needed to accommodate changes in your life or financial circumstances. This might include increasing your savings rate, adjusting your investment strategy, or revising your goals.

Preparing for Retirement

Retirement planning is crucial to ensure you have the financial resources to live comfortably after you stop working. It involves saving and investing over a long period to build a substantial retirement fund.

Start Early: The earlier you start saving for retirement, the better. Starting early gives your money more time to grow through compound interest. Even small contributions can grow significantly over time if invested wisely.

Contribute to Retirement Accounts: Take advantage of retirement accounts like 401(k)s, IRAs, and Roth IRAs. These accounts offer tax benefits that can help your savings grow more efficiently. Contribute as much as you can and take advantage of employer matching contributions if available.

Diversify Investments: Diversifying your investments helps spread risk and increase potential returns. Invest in a mix of assets, such as stocks, bonds, and real estate. This ensures that your retirement savings are not overly dependent on the performance of a single asset class.

Plan for Healthcare: Healthcare costs can be a significant expense in retirement. Consider options like long-term care insurance and Medicare to cover potential healthcare expenses. Include these costs in your retirement planning to ensure you have sufficient funds to cover them.

Leaving a Financial Legacy

Leaving a financial legacy involves planning to ensure your wealth benefits your family and future generations. It requires thoughtful estate planning and financial management.

Create a Will and Trust: A will outlines how your assets will be distributed after your death. It is essential to have a legally binding will to ensure your wishes are followed. A trust can help manage your assets, reduce estate taxes, and provide for your family.

Estate Planning: Work with an estate planner to develop a comprehensive estate plan. This includes setting up trusts, planning for taxes, and ensuring your assets are distributed according to your wishes. Estate planning helps protect your wealth and provide for your family.

Charitable Giving: Consider including charitable giving in your legacy plan. This allows you to support causes you care about and leave a positive impact. Charitable donations can also provide tax benefits, reducing the overall tax burden on your estate.

Educating Future Generations: Passing on financial knowledge is an essential part of leaving a legacy. Teach your children and grandchildren about money management, saving, and investing. This ensures they can continue to build on the financial foundation you have established.

Conclusion

Achieving financial freedom and building a secure future might seem daunting, but with the right strategies and disciplined approach, it's entirely possible. Velocity banking and effective financial management are powerful tools that can help you take control of your finances, reduce debt, and grow your wealth over time. By understanding the principles of velocity banking, setting clear financial goals, and maintaining a positive cash flow, you can pave the way to a more secure and prosperous future.

Remember, the journey to financial freedom is a marathon, not a sprint. It requires patience, persistence, and continuous learning. As you implement the strategies discussed in this book, you'll start to see the positive impact on your financial health. Stay committed to your goals, adapt to changes, and keep refining your financial plan.

Call to Action

Now that you have a comprehensive understanding of velocity banking and financial management, it's time to take action. Here are some steps to get started:

- **Assess Your Finances**: Take a close look at your income, expenses, and debts. Create a detailed financial statement to understand where you stand.
- **Set Clear Goals**: Define your short-term and long-term financial goals. Make sure they are specific, measurable, achievable, relevant, and time-bound (SMART).
- **Create a Budget**: Develop a budget that aligns with your financial goals. Track your spending, manage your expenses, and prioritize savings and debt repayment.

- **Implement Velocity Banking**: If you have high-interest debt, <u>consider using a HELOC or line of credit to pay it off faster</u>. Follow the steps outlined in this book to implement velocity banking effectively.
- **Monitor Your Progress**: Regularly review your financial plan and track your progress. Adjust your strategy as needed to stay on track and achieve your goals.
- **Seek Professional Advice**: If you need additional guidance, consider consulting with a financial advisor. Professional advice can help you make informed

decisions and optimize your financial strategy.

Taking control of your finances is an empowering journey. By applying the principles of velocity banking and sound financial management, you can achieve financial freedom and build a secure future for yourself and your loved ones. Start today, stay committed, and watch your financial health improve!

About the Author

H. N. Williams is a full-time stay-at-home mom passionate about financial literacy and management. She has an MBA from Western Governors University in Nevada and a Bachelor's in Applied Management from Grand Canyon University in Phoenix, Arizona. With her academic and practical experience, she empowers readers to master their finances and achieve financial freedom.

www.ingramcontent.com/pod-product-compliance
Lightning Source LLC
Chambersburg PA
CBHW071430220526
45469CB00004B/1475